ENOUGH,
dammit

a cynic's guide to finally getting
what you want out of life

karen salmansohn

CELESTIAL ARTS
Berkeley | Toronto

Copyright © 2004 by Karen Salmansohn
Photography and illustrations copyright © 2004 by Don Zinzell

A Kirsty Melville Book

Celestial Arts
PO Box 7123
Berkeley, California 94707
www.tenspeed.com

Distributed in Australia by Simon and Schuster Australia, in Canada by Ten Speed Press Canada, in New Zealand by Southern Publishers Group, in South Africa by Real Books, and in the United Kingdom and Europe by Airlift Book Company.

Concept and book packaging by Karen Salmansohn — www.notsalmon.com
Cover and book design by Zinzell — www.zinzell.com
Design Assistant: Virginie Boix

Library of Congress Cataloging-in-Publication Data
Salmansohn, Karen.
Enough, dammit : a cynic's guide to finally getting what you want out of life /
Karen Salmansohn.
p. cm.
"A Kirsty Melville book."
ISBN 1-58761-220-8 (pbk.)
1. Success — Psychological aspects. I. Title.
BF637.S8S25   2004
158.1—dc22   2004008149

First printing, 2004
Printed in Singapore

1 2 3 4 5 6 7 8 9 10 — 08 07 06 05 04

THE IDEA FOR THIS BOOK:
To create a self-help book that uses playful, easy-to-understand analogies and graphics to explain serious, complicated life theories (from Modern Cognitive Psychology, Sigmund Freud, Carl Jung, Sociology, Biology, Eastern Philosophy, Darwinism, Quantum Physics, the Zen of Enchiladas…and then some) so it's actually fun and possible to finally figure how to take control of your swerving, careening life.

WARNING #1:

You must always make sure that it is your true inner passion that is driving you forward in life. **EXTERNALLY DRIVEN PEOPLE WILL ALWAYS CRASH AND BURN!** This book will check for hidden defects in your motivating drive.

WARNING #2:

"Whatever you are, be a good one."

—Abraham Lincoln

You

don't like to
think of yourself
as a grown up…

but as a "growing up."

You want to always be growing…

...and
growing.

After all…
growing is a sign you are
fully alive and thriving.

And you know
what keeps you
fully alive, thriving,
growing…

when you are being
honest with yourself
and bravely following your heart.

Just as some of us were put
here to be doctors…some of
us to be musicians…some
of us to be full-time mothers…
(and at least one of us was put
here to invent that doohickey
that holds up the lid on the
pizza box!)…you have been
put here to do what you do
best…live your passions to
their fullest.

Which brings you to…

LIFE LESSON #1

The purpose of your life is to find and do the purpose **of your life...**

or what you like to call your DREAM QUEST.

Birds gotta fly. Fish gotta swim.
Dancers gotta dance. Business
owners gotta own businesses.

Gardeners gotta garden.

Mothers gotta mother.
Ice sculptors gotta make
ice sculptures. You gotta

_____

(fill in the blank with
your Dream Quest.)

And you know as surely as the Wright brothers, against all odds, lived out their passions to make certain our planet had flying winged steel vehicles (then, later, tiny aluminum pouches of peanuts)…you too will do what you can to make sure your Dream Quest flies.

Sure, your Dream Quest might have set off buoyantly a few times already...then crashed a few times already...then again... so did the Wright brothers' planes crash at first.

And heck, if the Wright brothers could eventually make a ton of steel fly through the air with the greatest of ease...it makes sense that it's possible for your Dream Quest to fly eventually too!

You just have to see obstacles the Wright way...with patience, focus, and optimism.

Which brings you to...

LIFE LESSON 02

Although life is unpredictable, **it does come with a 100% GUARANTEE.**

LIFE'S 100% GUARANTEE: While on your path heading toward your Dream Quest, you will 100% be bombarded with a series of obstacles that will make you mutter, "What the %$#! is going on here? I need a nap!"

Or as Dorothy once said,
"Lions and tigers and bears, oh my!"

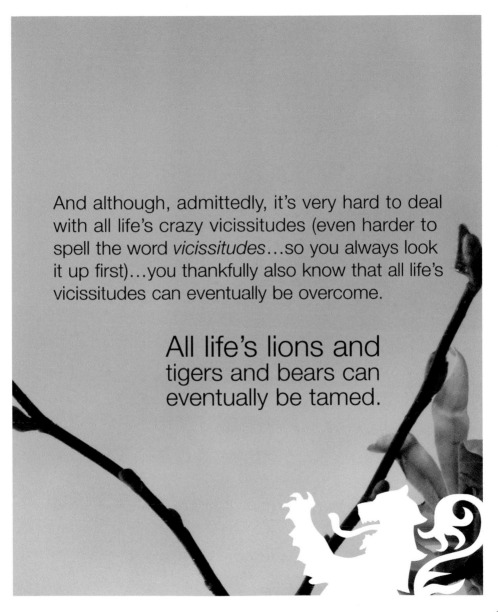

And although, admittedly, it's very hard to deal with all life's crazy vicissitudes (even harder to spell the word *vicissitudes*...so you always look it up first)...you thankfully also know that all life's vicissitudes can eventually be overcome.

All life's lions and tigers and bears can eventually be tamed.

You know it helps if you remember…
all achievements were at one time but a mere
"dream bubble" floating above a dreamer's
head that the dreamer kept on believing in
soooo much that eventually the dream had
no choice but to become a reality.

There's no
such person as
"LUCKY SO-AND-SO."
Every "LUCKY SO-AND-SO" was at one time
"A VERY-MUCH-TESTED-SO-AND-SO" who had faith
that The Universe would provide…
and thereby kept on pursuing
their Dream Quest.

For example, Rocky didn't go into the fight thinking, "Geez, I might not win!"

Then there's Sylvestor Stallone himself. He didn't go into the movie business thinking, "I'm just some chump from south Philly with great pecs. What do I know about film?"

No, Stallone believed passionately in his Dream Quest of making a great film…and therefore make a great film he did.

Which brings you to…

LIFE LESSON 03

There is no rational reason to remain a pessimist in a world that is full of so many miracles!

YO: The Wright brothers flew a plane!

A guy with great pecs from South Philly made a film that garnered awards and gazillions of dollars!

A broke single mom created the international success of Harry Potter and became one of the most respected, wealthiest people in the world!

Are you going to insult this complex, infinite miracle-making machine called The Universe with your lack of belief in its grand abundance to provide you with what you need?

You don't think so!

Which brings you to…

LIFE LESSON

04

Lots of pessimism will never get you what you want. Lots of pessimism will only get you lots of opportunity to be right about your pessimism.

You don't want to be a pessimist who succeeds at being right about your pessimism.

You want to be an optimist who succeeds at success.

Which reminds you of a quote from Henry Ford: "If you think you can do a thing or think you cannot do a thing, you're right."

You know Henry is right.

You know that if you allow yourself to foolishly believe that you will never be happily married, never be professionally successful, never be sexy as the dickens, you foolishly never will be!

Which brings you to...

LIFE LESSON 05

There are many psychological reasons for why negative thinking brings negative life circumstances.

Luckily you can sum them all up in one simple sentence: Your psychological beliefs create your daily habits that create your life circumstances.

Luckily you can also sum all that up in one simple metaphor:

Just as daisy seeds will always grow daisies… negative thought seeds (despair, blame, regret, fear, anger, shame, guilt, resentment, self-pity, hate) will always grow negative habits that will then grow into negative life circumstances.

Similarly, positive thought seeds (faith, love, harmony, creativity, kindness, peace, forgiveness, acceptance, enthusiasm, discipline, bliss, abundance mentality) will always grow positive habits that will grow into positive life circumstances.

Your psychological problem:

Sometimes the seeds of your negative beliefs are buried in your subconscious mind...planted so deep in your lower consciousness that you're not even aware they're down there...

and so you can wind up growing
lots-of weedy negative
life circumstances
you didn't even know you
planted in the first place.

More dirt on your thought seeds:

Your lower consciousness seems to have the ideal dark and musty climate for negative thought seeds to grow. So, if you want to ensure you don't grow a jungle of negative life circumstances, you've got to prune and nurture the garden of your subconscious mind on a regular basis.

You've got to conscientiously pluck out any negative thought seeds the moment you find them — before they grow untamable! And as for whatever weedy negative life circumstances you already have growing in your life, you must be sure to pull them all out by their deepest roots...so they don't grow back in again when you're not looking.

Which brings you to...

LIFE LESSON 06

You recognize there are also spiritual and scientific reasons why negative thinking brings negative life circumstances.

Luckily you can also sum all them up in one simple sentence:
Many Spiritual Theorists and Quantum Physicists believe that thoughts are a form of vibrating energy that attract similarly vibrating energy fields (i.e., people and circumstances) accordingly.

Luckily you can also sum all that up in a simple metaphor:
Thoughts work like magnets. You attract what you think.

Hence:
Synchronicity exists.
Nothing is random.

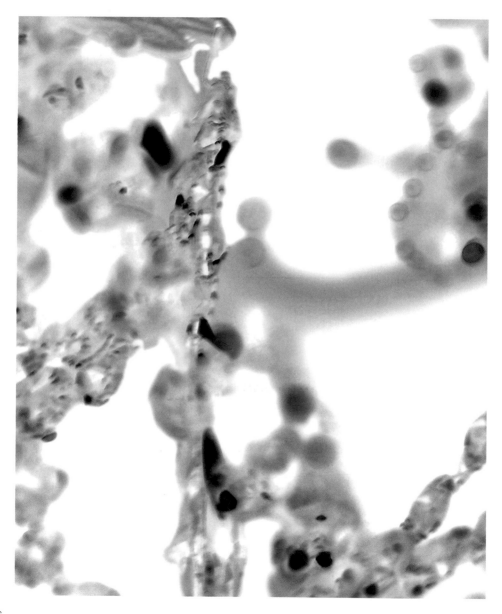

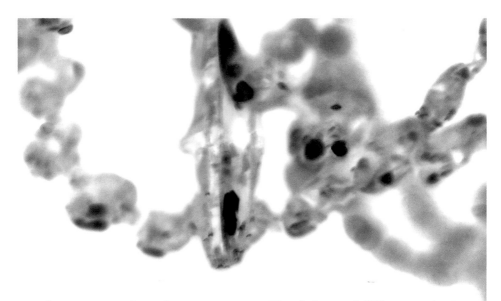

Interestingly, many Spiritual Theorists and Quantum Physicists also believe that if you consistently think positive thoughts you will not only attract more positivity…

you will raise your thought frequency to what some call Spirit Energy…and some call Higher Consciousness…a level so high in vibration that it supposedly connects to the energy of the entire universe…or what Albert Einstein called "Infinite Intelligence"… what Einstein believed to be a humongous invisible thought ocean where all the answers you've ever tried to look for can be found.

When you think about the Infinite Intelligence that Spirit Energy offers you're reminded of something else you once read…about how the word *inspire* literally translates into…**"in spirit"**…which now makes total sense.

When you are inspired (INSPIRED TO UNTANGLE A PROBLEM, INSPIRED TO CREATE A WORK OF ART, INSPIRED TO DO AN ACT OF KINDNESS) you now realize it's because you are plugged into this

Spirit Energy!

Which brings you to…

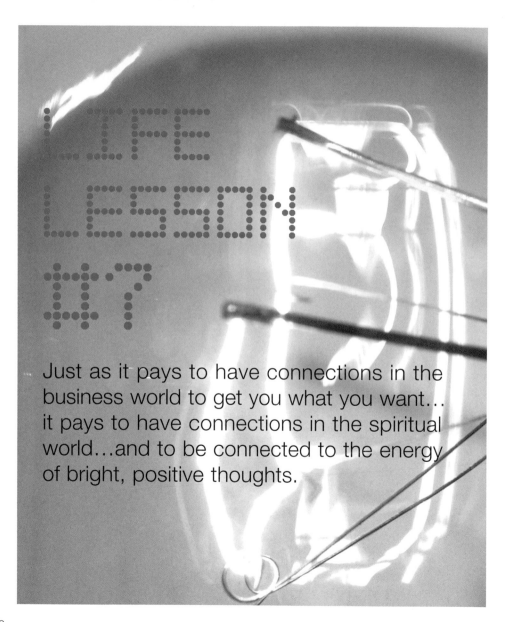

LIFE LESSON #7

Just as it pays to have connections in the business world to get you what you want... it pays to have connections in the spiritual world...and to be connected to the energy of bright, positive thoughts.

It's as if this "bright, positive thought energy" sheds light on hidden answers. And when you become unplugged…that's when more mistakes and problems arise, because…well…when you can't see clearly in the dark, you wind up breaking your self-promises, stepping all over your hopes, squooshing your dreams.

Thankfully you now know WHY you sometimes wind up in the dark.

Which brings you to…

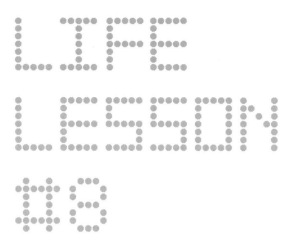

LIFE LESSON #8

Throughout the years you have been brainwashed by all kinds of negative beliefs about love, success, money, etc. Although it's more like you've been braindirtied.

Basically, over time, your lens for seeing the world has become very muddied up with negative, dark beliefs about: despair, regret, shame, guilt, resentment, self-pity, hate, fear, anger!

And so it is this braindirtied build-up that makes the world appear so dark and un-navigable!

Alas,

sometimes the world appears sooooooo dark...
that you are unable to see that you could easily
plug into Spirit Energy and thereby easily
get the guiding light you need.

And...so...because you
don't have access to your
Plan A guiding light of
Spirit Energy, you turn to
Plan B: relying on your
subconscious as a guide.

The problem:
your subconscious
is a lousy guide!

Your subconscious is what
braindirtied you up in the
first place by allowing all
those dark beliefs to collect.

And because your subconscious can't see the
world rightly, it can't see any new, improved paths
that would lead you to a new, better place.

So, instead your subconscious leads you down
the paths it already knows…hence you sometimes
find yourself going down the same old negative
paths…like HEARTBREAK LANE, NOT-SO-EASY
STREET, DISAPPOINTMENT HIGHWAY…
again and again.

Although you know this sounds
rather nutty of your subconscious,
you also know this to be so.

HOW YOUR NUTTY LITTLE LIFE WORKS IN A NUTSHELL:

You aim yourself toward what your subconscious has learned to be the map of the world… not toward what you consciously want and all the world truly offers.

Which brings you to…

 **LIFE LESSON 09**

You must make sure you live in the present and stop reliving the past. And you know from reading Freud that you have two ways to relive your past:

1. Through your memories.
2. Through your actions.

Meaning, you can relive your past by:

1. Overdoing your daily thoughts
about your past.
2. Choosing current situations
that are doppelgangers to your
past…being led to these familiar
reenactments by the urgings of
your braindirtied subconscious mind.

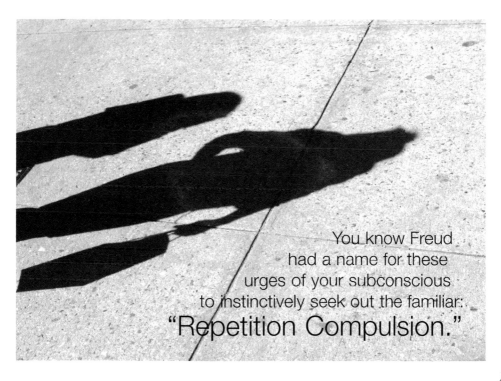

You know Freud
had a name for these
urges of your subconscious
to instinctively seek out the familiar:
"Repetition Compulsion."

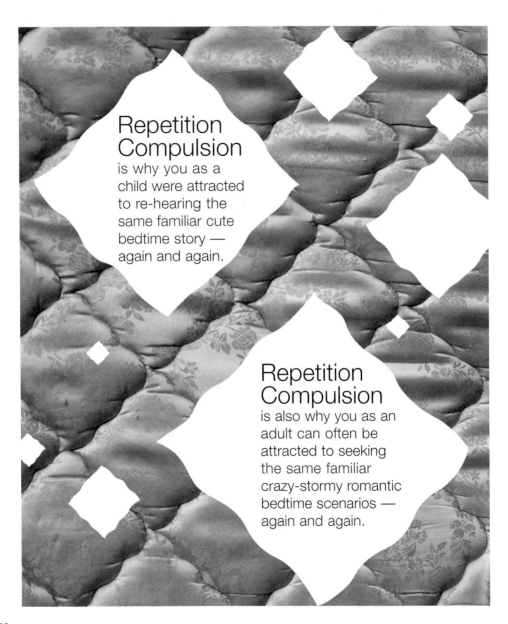

Repetition Compulsion
is why you as a child were attracted to re-hearing the same familiar cute bedtime story — again and again.

Repetition Compulsion
is also why you as an adult can often be attracted to seeking the same familiar crazy-stormy romantic bedtime scenarios — again and again.

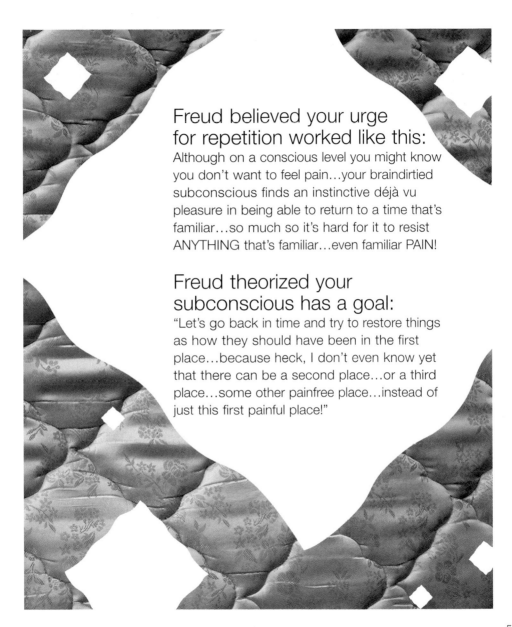

Freud believed your urge for repetition worked like this:

Although on a conscious level you might know you don't want to feel pain…your braindirtied subconscious finds an instinctive déjà vu pleasure in being able to return to a time that's familiar…so much so it's hard for it to resist ANYTHING that's familiar…even familiar PAIN!

Freud theorized your subconscious has a goal:

"Let's go back in time and try to restore things as how they should have been in the first place…because heck, I don't even know yet that there can be a second place…or a third place…some other painfree place…instead of just this first painful place!"

When you think about all this, you're reminded of something you once read in a big, thick boring book on modern-day cognitive therapy.

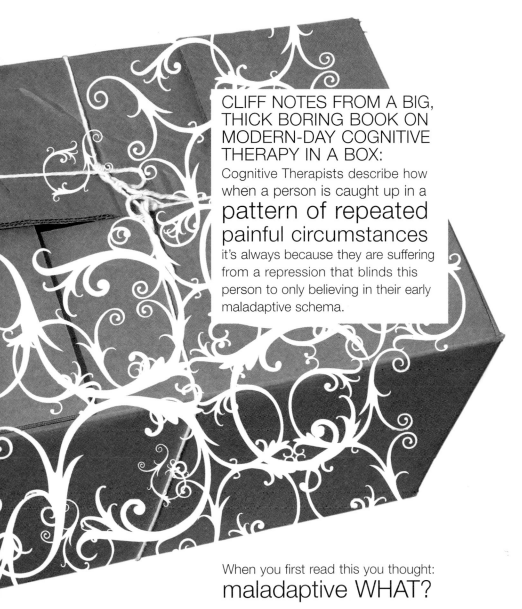

CLIFF NOTES FROM A BIG, THICK BORING BOOK ON MODERN-DAY COGNITIVE THERAPY IN A BOX:
Cognitive Therapists describe how when a person is caught up in a **pattern of repeated painful circumstances** it's always because they are suffering from a repression that blinds this person to only believing in their early maladaptive schema.

When you first read this you thought:
maladaptive WHAT?

Then thankfully the big, boring book explained this a bit more:

If you grew up being mentally or physically abused by a parent, you will develop an "early maladaptive schema" that you are "unlovable" — and then be led by your subconscious into craving **patterns of pain** until you finally dump your "early maladaptive schema."

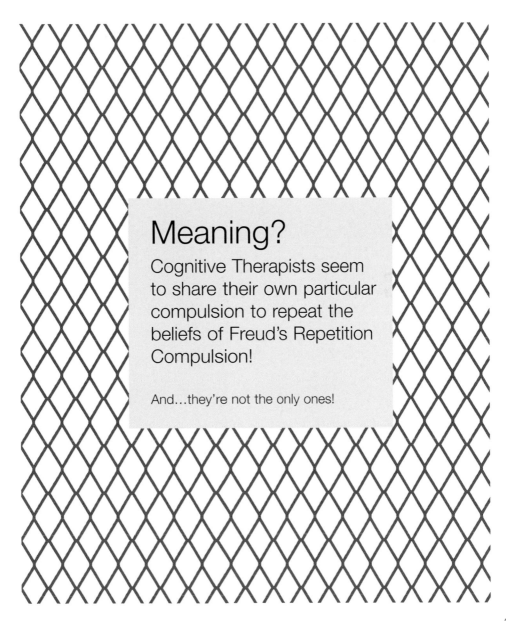

Meaning?

Cognitive Therapists seem to share their own particular compulsion to repeat the beliefs of Freud's Repetition Compulsion!

And...they're not the only ones!

What Freud calls "Repetition Compulsion" and Cognitive Therapists call "Maladaptive Schema" you call a "Portable Childhood"… which is basically your belief that you seem to have this self-torturing urge to carry your

heavy childhood baggage

with you wherever you go…
to the office…into
a relationship.

YOUR PORTABLE CHILDHOOD THEORY FURTHER EXPLAINED:

Wherever you may be, however old you are, you reenact your childhood drama with whomever you handily have around. You can cast a colleague in the Daddy Role or a friend in the Mommy Dearest Role. For example, you might purposefully choose a friend who is late to meet you because you had a mother who was always late to pick you up from school, and then when your friend is late, your friend's tardiness would then trigger an anger response within you that's stronger than your friend deserves because of your portable childhood reenactment triggers. You're again pissed off that Mother was late — and again you will yell at your friend/mother in hopes of changing this behavior — so you can feel lovable and worthy, because tardiness for you means unlovability and unworthiness.

And so you stop to think about your urg
for déjà vu past pain…and that's when
you're reminded of the love
pattern of your past…
your old pattern for
craving pain-bearing
paramours!

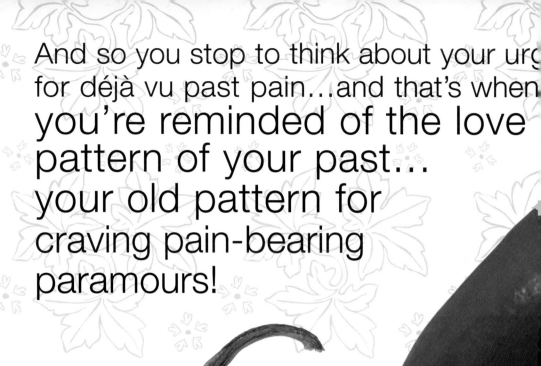

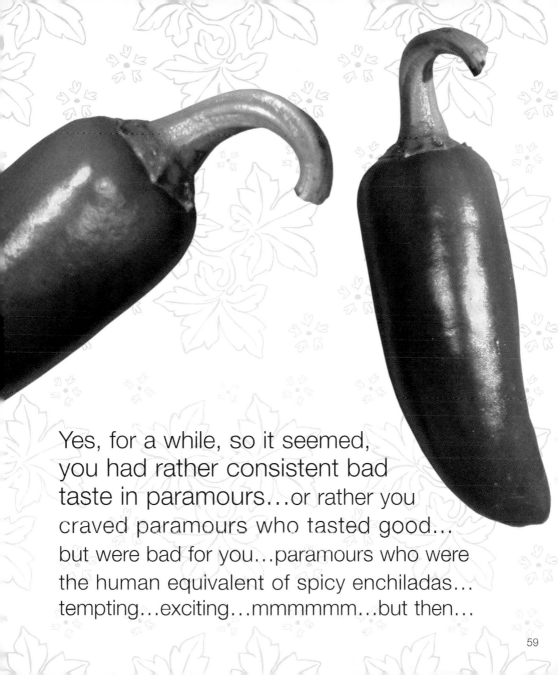

Yes, for a while, so it seemed,
you had rather consistent bad
taste in paramours…or rather you
craved paramours who tasted good…
but were bad for you…paramours who were
the human equivalent of spicy enchiladas…
tempting…exciting…mmmmmm…but then…

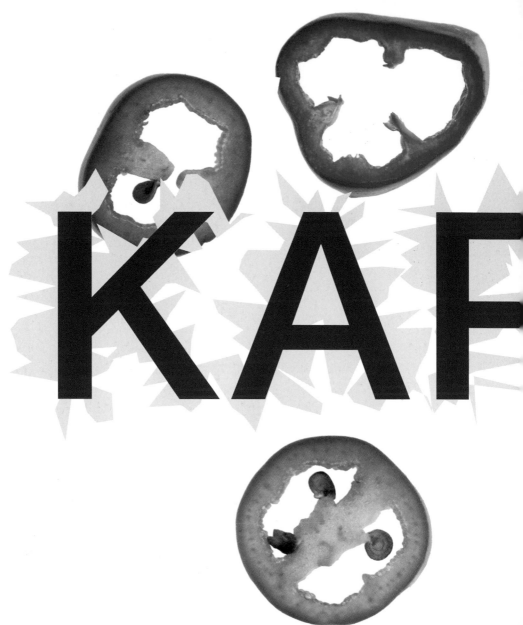

KAF

POW

...these paramours would suddenly become a disruptive influence on your entire system.

But just like you loved your spicy enchiladas...and didn't want to give them up...you didn't want to give up your spicy enchilada paramours either...and so you kept on having repeated heartache.

Until one day you realized...

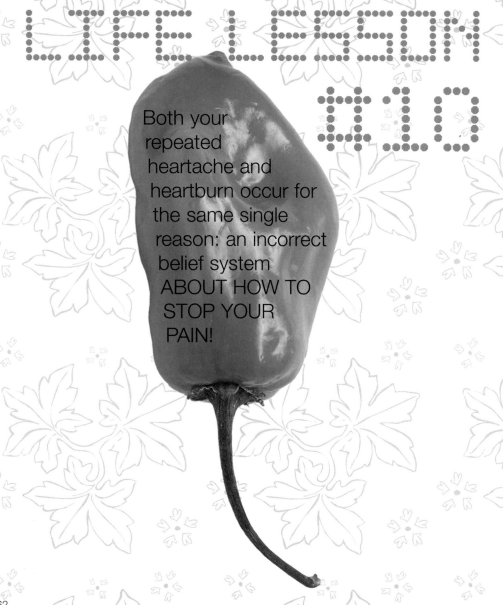

LIFE LESSON #10

Both your repeated heartache and heartburn occur for the same single reason: an incorrect belief system ABOUT HOW TO STOP YOUR PAIN!

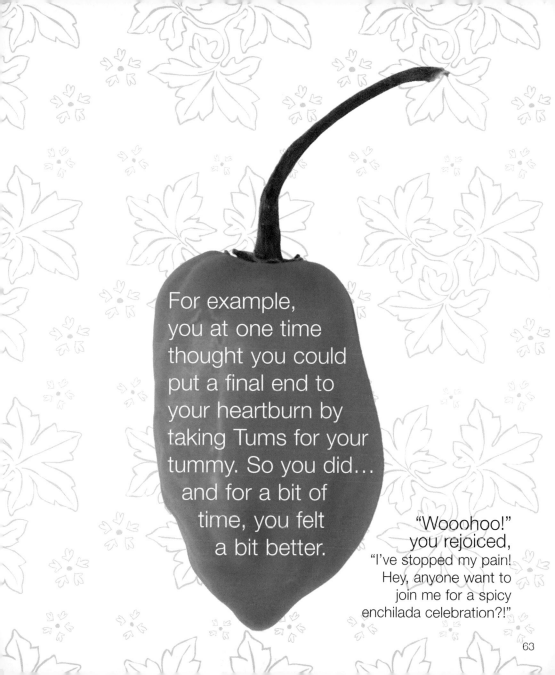

For example, you at one time thought you could put a final end to your heartburn by taking Tums for your tummy. So you did... and for a bit of time, you felt a bit better.

"Wooohoo!" you rejoiced, "I've stopped my pain! Hey, anyone want to join me for a spicy enchilada celebration?!"

Next thing you knew:

WHA

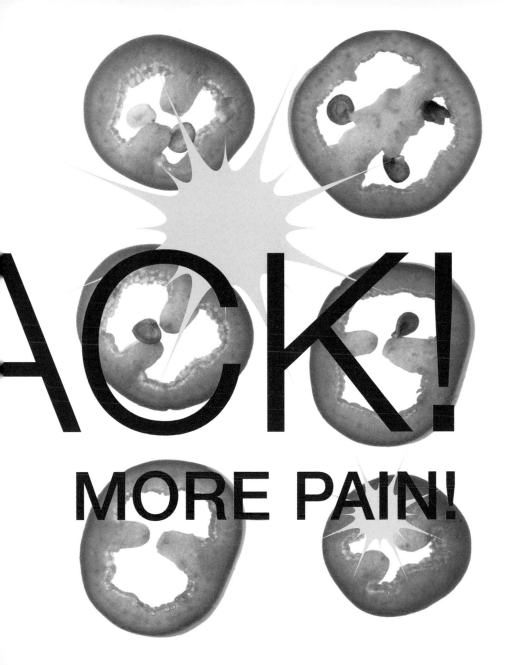

ACK!
MORE PAIN!

"Hmm," you thought. "Tums didn't work...
I'll try Pepto instead!

Again: WHACK!
MORE PAIN!

"Hmm," you thought. "Maybe Alka Seltzer will do the trick!"

Again: MORE PAIN!

And the same pattern of pain went for your pattern of paramours.

"Dating Tom didn't work," you told yourself, "so I'll try dating Pete."

Later, again: WHACK! MORE PAIN!

"Pete didn't work, I'll try dating Al."

Later, again: WHACK! MORE PAIN!

Finally you realized changing from Tums to Pepto or Tom to Pete was not the answer!

Which brings you to...

LIFE LESSON #11

IF YOU WANT TO STOP YOUR
RECURRING PAIN FOR GOOD YOU
MUST FIRST CORRECTLY SEE WHAT
YOU ARE DOING BAD!

YOU MUST CORRECTLY SEE THE
DIFFERENCE BETWEEN "THE CAUSE
OF YOUR ORIGINAL PAIN" AND "THE
EFFECTS OF YOUR ORIGINAL PAIN."

THE CAUSE OF YOUR ORIGINAL PAIN:
your repetition compulsion for pain-bearing
spicy enchiladas/pain-bearing spicy
paramours

THE EFFECTS OF YOUR ORIGINAL PAIN:
heartburn/heartache

NOW YOU KNOW:
If you want to break free from the alluring spell of REPETITION COMPULSION, break free from your MALADAPTIVE SCHEMA, break free from your PORTABLE CHILDHOOD, break free from your subconscious BRAINDIRTIED NEGATIVE URGES TO SEEK OUT FAMILIAR PAIN AGAIN AND AGAIN — you must hunt down and say ENOUGH, DAMMIT to the "CAUSE of your original pain"…that original braindirtying event that created the dark lens you now have of the world. Then you must clean up your lens…

so it's nice and clear and lucid!

A DETAILED EXAMPLE IN A BOX:

1. You must find your original cause of pain that first created your darkened braindirtied self-destructive belief that: "Spicy food and spicy paramours are yummy and fun…I've been indulging in them all my life and I just love 'em!"

2. You must then wipe, wipe, wipe away this braindirtied belief until you can finally see clearly: "There are many non-spicy-non-pain-bearing yummy options out there! The spicy-pain-bearing menu I was fed in childhood is NOT the ONLY menu in town!"

Which brings you to…

WARNING:

IF you only change "the effects of your pain"…change from Tums to Pepto to Alka Seltzer…change from dating Tom to Pete to Al…you will keep on re-experiencing recurring pain because you'll keep on having the same cravings for pain…the same REPETITION COMPULSION.

Which brings you to…

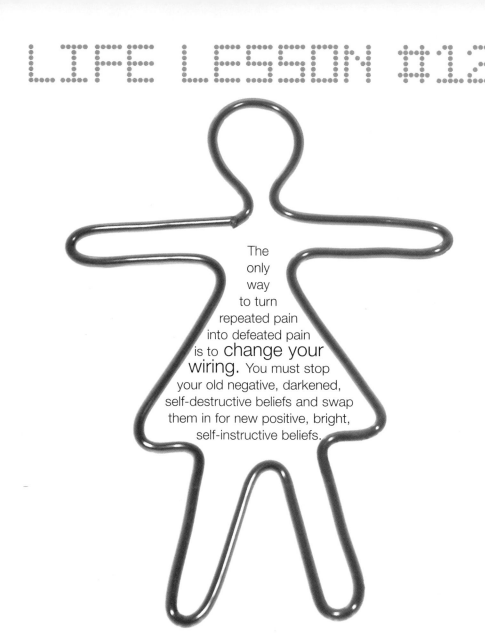

The
only
way
to turn
repeated pain
into defeated pain
is to change your
wiring. You must stop
your old negative, darkened,
self-destructive beliefs and swap
them in for new positive, bright,
self-instructive beliefs.

Of course you recognize stopping and swapping your learned beliefs is not so simple...because alas, you are human and thereby very complicated.

Yes, you as a human have some very complicated wiring that's been miswired since childhood.

Your problem:

rewiring and replugging your wiring is not only time consuming...but VERY, VERY scary!

Rewiring and replugging
might give you a SHOCK!

And in fact, you are right to think you'll be shocked.

When you rewire and replug yourself, you will always experience momentary SHOCKS OF TRUTHS...as well as the glaring painful light of self-responsibility in your face.

Um...er...which is why you've been preferring to stay in the dark. You've been choosing to stay with your PATTERN OF FAMILIAR PAIN rather than risk the POTENTIAL NEW PAIN from shocking truths and the glaring light of self-responsibility.

Which brings you to...

LIFE LESSON #13

If you want to get out of the darkness you are in, you must be willing to experience momentary shock and glare.

Yes, just as when you've been in a dark room and turn on the light, your eyes will always initially sting, the same goes for being in the emotional dark and turning on your guiding light.

THE GOOD NEWS IS:
Although this shock and glare might hurt at first...
the illumination you receive from truth and
self-responsibility will always help you find new,
unexplored paths that can lead you to your
Dream Quest.

THE BAD NEWS IS:
If you don't bother to rewire and replug yourself...
The Universe will attempt to do it for you...
by giving you SOME VERY LARGE SHOCKS!

This is sooo important to keep in mind...
it deserves its own life lesson...

Which brings you to...

LIFE LESSON #14

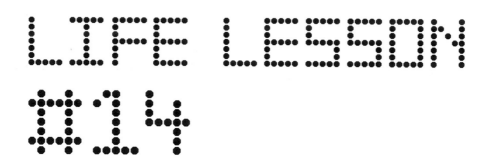

If you don't bother to rewire and replug yourself, this complicated machinery called The Universe will do it for you by giving you many **SHOCKING EXPERIENCES** hoping to jolt you out of your **REPETITION COMPULSION TRANCE**…and jumpstart you to restart your life again…with a new better start.

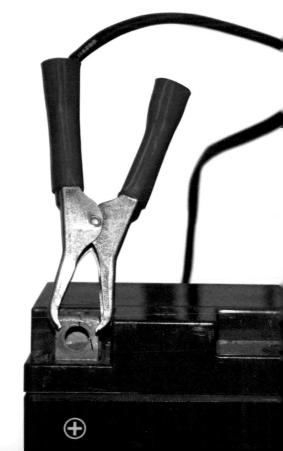

It's like this:

The Universe knows there is a better way to live than with your incorrect, incomplete, negative, braindirtied beliefs. And so The Universe tries to WAKE YOU UP FROM YOUR REPETITION COMPULSION TRANCE… by giving you SHOCKS OF PAIN…and it need be A VERY BIG EMERGENCY SHOCK OF CRISIS PAIN.

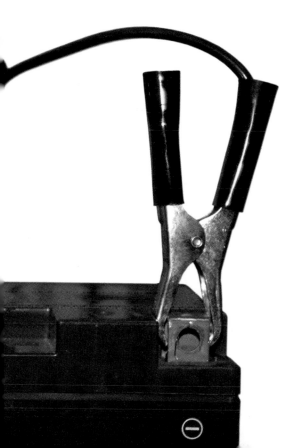

For example:

The Universe might give you a scary, psychopathically bad love relationship, which leads you to realize ENOUGH WITH PAIN-BEARING PEOPLE, DAMMIT! I NOW SEE I MUST STOP MY SELF-DESTRUCTIVE LEARNED BELIEF THAT "PAIN-BEARING PARAMOURS ARE FUN AND YUMMY!" AND SWAP IT IN FOR A SELF-INSTRUCTIVE POSITIVE BELIEF THAT "THERE ARE OTHER BETTER-FOR-ME PARAMOURS OUT THERE THAT ARE FUNNER AND YUMMIER!!"

Which brings you to…

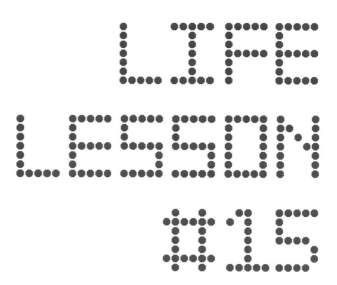

LIFE LESSON #15

PAIN IS YOUR EVOLUTIONARY BUDDY…
a highly effective "Please Evolve NOW Prompter"
to get you to go with the Darwinian program and
evolve, baby, evolve.

And whenever you experience crisis pain — that
major nightmare event in your life — this is always
The Universe's emergency effort to WAKE YOU
UP from your Repetition Compulsion slumber.

Yes, you're never meant to lose yourself in your pain. Quite the opposite. You're meant to find yourself in your pain…your true inner self…your Spirit Energy self… your Higher Consciousness self.

Yes indeedie, the number one purpose of pain is to get you to (finally!) (boldly!) look deep, deep inside yourself — where you will find your 100% original-flavored most powerful true you… the one without all those artificial ingredients like doubt, fear, worry, angst, insecurity, hopelessness, despair. And it's this 100% pure Spirit Energy, 100% clearly seeing you that will ultimately lead you to your Dream Quest!

Nutrition Facts

Serving Size 1/2 tsp (2g)
Servings Per Container about 1

Amount Per Serving

Calories 150

	% Daily Value*
Fear 93mg	**99%**
Total Worry 86mg	**100%**
Angst 85mg	**99%**
Total Hopelessness 62mg	**97%**
Insecurity 97mg	**95%**

Despair 100%

* Percent Daily Values are based on a 2,000 calorie diet.

Which reminds you of a story about a guy named Ralph...

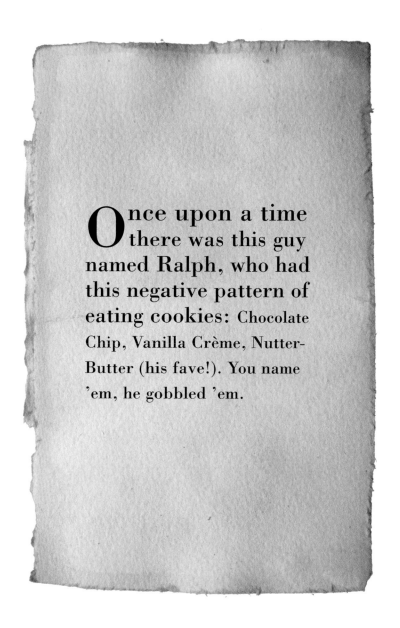

Once upon a time there was this guy named Ralph, who had this negative pattern of eating cookies: Chocolate Chip, Vanilla Crème, Nutter-Butter (his fave!). You name 'em, he gobbled 'em.

Soon, Ralph became on the rotund side. Translation: Ralph became as fat as a house…and a very big house, not just one of those tiny cottages in a small village.

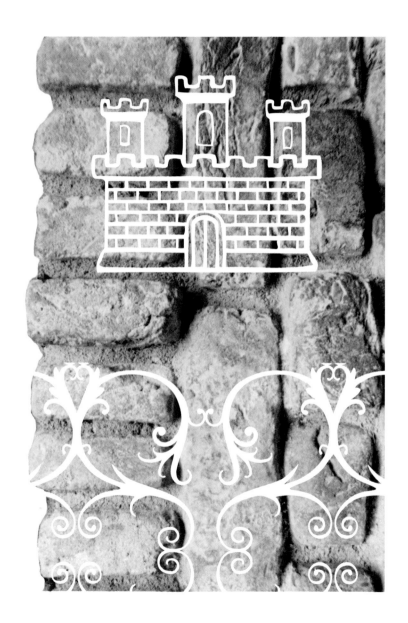

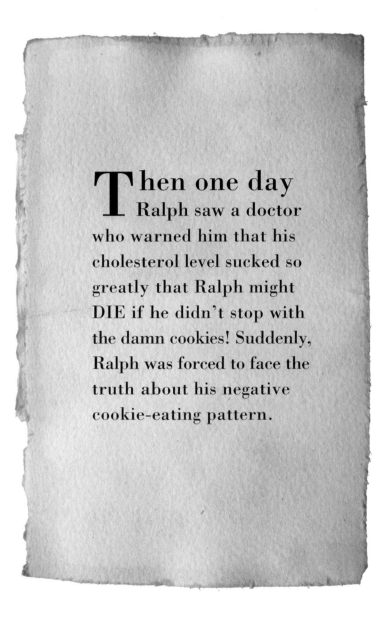

Then one day Ralph saw a doctor who warned him that his cholesterol level sucked so greatly that Ralph might DIE if he didn't stop with the damn cookies! Suddenly, Ralph was forced to face the truth about his negative cookie-eating pattern.

When Ralph listened closely to what his cholesterol-gasping heart had to say, Ralph heard it tell him all about his Original Source of Pain…Ralph's Fear of Being Abandoned If Ralph Were To Be Thin Enough To Feel Good Enough To Fall In Love Which Came About Because Ralph's Mother Passed Away When He Was Nine Which Is Something Ralph Does Not Like To Think About And Would Rather Eat Cookies Instead, Dammit.

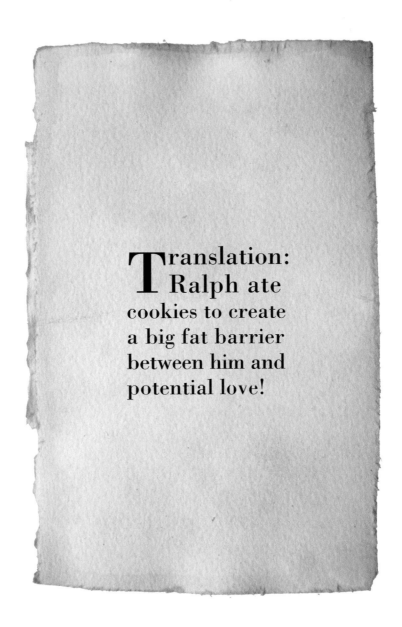

Translation: Ralph ate cookies to create a big fat barrier between him and potential love!

But now Ralph had a fear greater than his Original Fear of Abandonment…he had Fear of Death. So out of desperation Ralph learned to swap his old negative thoughts about "love leading to abandonment and his not being worthy of love" for new positive thoughts about "wanting to stay alive and not die like his mother did so he could break this family pattern and carry on the family lineage and hmmm…maybe his mother passed away not because she did not love him…maybe she was just sick…and maybe he is loveworthy and won't be abandoned if he falls in love with something other than Nutter-Butter Cookies!"

Soon after, Ralph told himself "Enough with cookies, dammit! I deserve love, dammit!"

Ralph realized he played a role in both his cholesterol problem and his lack of love problem… and it was up to him to make a swap of negative beliefs about love and his original maternal love and his present lack of any love!

It was up to him to make a swap of cookies for salad…all of which led Ralph to finally find the love of his dreams in the form of a girl named Trixie whom he met at a salad bar fighting with those metal tongs over a particularly ripe tomato. Trixie gave Ralph the tomato. Ralph gave Trixie some carats! And they lived happily, dreamily ever after.

You know the lesson to be learned from Ralph:

Often it takes CRISIS PAIN to strike for you to change because CRISIS PAIN suddenly makes your fear of all that NEW POTENTIAL PAIN from shock and glare suddenly look a lot less scary.

Which brings you to…

LIFE LESSON #16

Although pain is one hell of a life-improvement teacher, you can self-teach yourself to rewire and replug your brain wiring…and thereby finally stop foolishly operating your mind on Auto-Pilot Repetition Compulsion Mode!

Yes, you CAN teach your old brain some new tricks.

Luckily you also know the first trick you must teach your brain… a little trick you call PUPPY TRAIN YOUR BRAIN.

PUPPY TRAIN YOUR BRAIN EXPLAINED:

Once, when you were at the doctor's, about to get a shot, the nurse told you not to think about the potential pain of the needle, but rather force your mind to think about something that makes you happy, like ADORABLE PUPPIES! And so you retrained your brain to think PUPPIES, PUPPIES, PUPPIES…not NEEDLE PAIN, NEEDLE PAIN, NEEDLE PAIN…and voilà, your needle pain be gone…or, at least, it was a heck of a lot less. You know the same holds true for your fear of POTENTIAL NEW PAIN FROM CHANGE. When you train your brain to refocus on something that makes you happy, like DREAM QUEST, DREAM QUEST, DREAM QUEST, instead of POTENTIAL NEW PAIN, POTENTIAL NEW PAIN, POTENTIAL NEW PAIN…voilà…potential new pain be gone… or, at least, it will be a heck of a lot less.

Which brings you to…

If you want to change
your life for the better,
you must change your mind's
mind about its view of change…
so it views change for the better!

You must STOP focusing on:
CHANGE = NEW POTENTIAL PAIN.

You must SWAP in focusing on:
CHANGE = SNAGGING YOUR
DREAM QUEST!

You must STOP focusing on:
CHANGE = DREAD

You must SWAP in focusing on:
CHANGE = EXCITEMENT OVER
ALL THAT WILL SOON BE YOURS!

Which brings you to...

LIFE LESSON #18

Because nature abhors a vacuum (almost as much as you abhor to vacuum), it's important that whenever you STOP an old negative belief, you also SWAP it…give your brain something new to grasp onto.

If you only SWEEP OUT and don't SWEEP IN...

well, then your brain will wind up feeling empty...and thereby immediately head on back to retrieve its old beliefs.

A STOP AND SWAP EXAMPLE:

If a sneaky negative thought enters your head:
"I'm afraid to change! I don't have the will not to eat this cookie! In fact, not eating cookies makes me feel pretty lousy, so why not eat just one little cookie…or…um…two…mmmm?"

You must consciously STOP IT AND SWAP IT for a positive thought:
"I'm psyched to change! I'm psyched to feel and look amazing. I wisely know that no matter how good eating a cookie may make me feel in the moment…nothing will ever make me feel as good as snagging my Dream Quest!"

MORE EXAMPLES OF STOP AND SWAP SWITCHEROOS:

Stop your negative thought:
I can't ask for that raise! My boss will laugh in my face.

Swap a positive thought:
I'm excited to make extra money and pay for my kid's future college education!

Stop your negative thought:
I'm too old to quit my career! It's so exhausting and painful!

Swap a positive thought:
My friend started a new career at 35 and she's sooo happy and fulfilled! I too want to feel happy and fulfilled!

And when you think about all the benefits of doing a stop and swap switcheroo, you realize stopping and swapping your belief about change is just the beginning of how stopping and swapping beliefs can give you a new life beginning.

Which brings you to…

LIFE LESSON #19

IF YOU WANT YOUR DAMN DREAMS TO COME TRUE YOU MUST FOLLOW A SPECIFIC PROGRAM OF 5 STOP AND SWAP SWITCHEROOS.

STOP AND SWAP SWITCHEROO #1 of 5
You need to swap a NEGATIVE closed mind
for a POSITIVE open mind.

STOP AND SWAP SWITCHEROO #2 of 5
You need to swap NEGATIVE acceptance
of a bummer of a life for a POSITIVE focus
on attaining your DREAM QUEST.

STOP AND SWAP SWITCHEROO #3 of 5
You need to swap NEGATIVE blame for
POSITIVE self-responsibility.

STOP AND SWAP SWITCHEROO #4 of 5
You need to swap NEGATIVE doubt for
POSITIVE faith.

STOP AND SWAP SWITCHEROO #5 of 5
You need to swap NEGATIVE laziness and
apathy for POSITIVE enthusiastic discipline.

And so you think more about these 5
STOP AND SWAP SWITCHEROOS...
and see how they all are important
life lessons unto themselves...

Which brings you to...

LIFE LESSON

You must believe in
THE POWER OF
STOP AND SWAP
SWITCHEROO #1 of 5.

You need to swap a NEGATIVE closed mind for a POSITIVE open mind…and seek out an alternate meaning for past patterns of pain and failure.

When you think about this, you're reminded of something else you once read in that big, fat boring book on cognitive therapy.

SOMETHING ELSE YOU ONCE READ IN THAT BIG, FAT BORING BOOK ON COGNITIVE THERAPY:
Cognitive Therapists all say that the secret to snagging success, happiness, and love is to get your negative-thought-chattering subconscious to shut up and take a hike. (Only, granted, those Cognitive Therapists didn't say it exactly like that.)

WHAT COGNITIVE THERAPISTS DID SAY:
Cognitive Therapists recommend a process called "collaborative empiricism" wherein the Cognitive Therapist loosens up the patient's "rigidity of mind" by suggesting new meanings about past pain.

AN EASY-TO-UNDERSTAND EXAMPLE:

MAYBE SOMEONE (BE IT MOM OR FRIEND) WHO SHOWS UP LATE TO MEET YOU ISN'T LATE BECAUSE YOU ARE UNLOVABLE AND UNWORTHY. MAYBE IT'S BECAUSE THIS PERSON IS WEIGHED DOWN BY THEIR OWN **EMOTIONAL BAGGAGE...** AND THAT SLOWS THEM DOWN TO MEET LOVEWORTHY, ADORABLE, FABULOUS YOU!

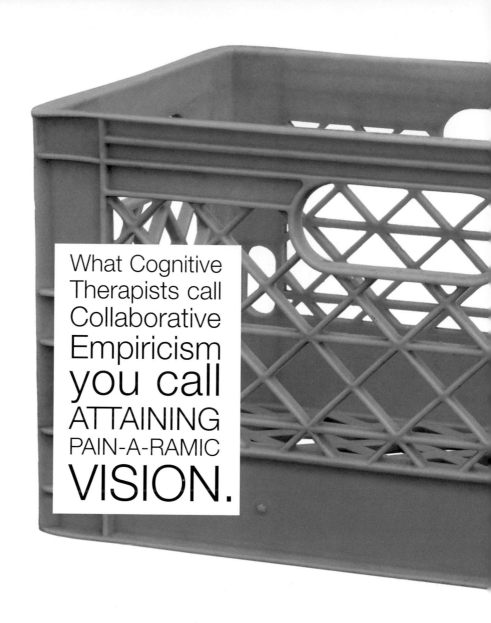

What Cognitive Therapists call Collaborative Empiricism you call ATTAINING PAIN-A-RAMIC VISION.

PAIN-A-RAMIC VISION EXPLAINED IN A BOX:
This is when you are able to flexibly, fully view pain from every angle, until you find a positive angle to lean on...an angle that will give you the positive boost you need to push yourself up, up, up, until you can see the world through the higher perspective of your Higher Consciousness.

AN EXAMPLE OF PAIN-A-RAMIC VISION AS A TOUR DE FORCE:

When Lance Armstrong got cancer he consciously decided to self-run his mind with PAIN-A-RAMIC VISION and see himself not as an "unlucky cancer victim" but as a "lucky cancer survivor" who learned lucky lessons that would help him achieve his DREAM QUEST of winning the Tour de France when he got out of the hospital. In particular, Lance wisely decided to see cancer as a helpful opportunity to teach himself the needed lesson of "interdependence," the lesson of allowing people to help him, which he'd never done before when he was cycling! The results? Post-cancer-survival Lance applied this lucky cancer lesson of "interdependence" to his cycling career, and finally allowed teammates to help him during the Tour de France…and so he finally became a total tour de force…and WON, WON, WON! His bout with cancer became about the lucky lesson he needed to learn… so his pain was morphed into gain. He consciously STOPPED focusing on being a victim of cancer and SWAPPED in refocusing on being a victor of his Dream Quest: winning the Tour de France!

Which brings you to…

LIFE LESSON

#21

You know seeing life with PAIN-A-RAMIC VISION is what successful, happy, loved/loving, always growing people do — and what you must do so you can join the crowd of successful, happy, loved/loving, always growing people.

Thankfully you now
even know how to attain
PAIN-A-RAMIC VISION.

HOW TO ATTAIN PAIN-A-RAMIC VISION:

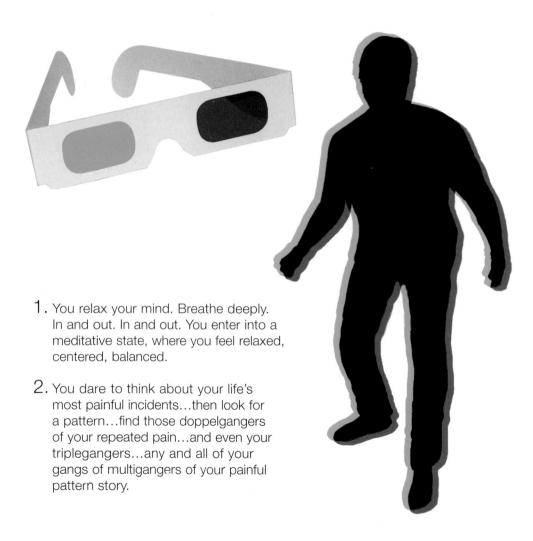

1. You relax your mind. Breathe deeply. In and out. In and out. You enter into a meditative state, where you feel relaxed, centered, balanced.

2. You dare to think about your life's most painful incidents…then look for a pattern…find those doppelgangers of your repeated pain…and even your triplegangers…any and all of your gangs of multigangers of your painful pattern story.

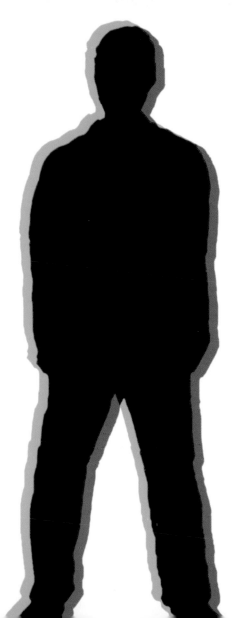

3. You try to find the original source from whence your repeated multigangers of pain all came from… that braindirtied dark place where your cravings for self-destructive Repetition Compulsion first got their start.

4. You force yourself to answer the following: WHAT IS A POSITIVE AND/OR LUCKY WAY TO EXPLAIN AND FIND GAIN FROM MY PAIN? You make a list of 5 POSITIVE MEANINGS FOR AND 5 POSITIVE LESSONS FROM YOUR PAIN.

5. You recognize that you have potential triggers that remind you of your pain and might thereby set off a downward spiral of negative thinking and behavior. So you clear your life of these potential triggers (i.e., remove those cookies from your cupboards! Remove those photos of your ex from your dashboard…and/or dartboard!).

Which brings you to…

You must believe in
THE POWER OF STOP AND SWAP
SWITCHEROO #2 of 5.

You need to swap NEGATIVE acceptance of a bummer of a life for a POSITIVE focus on attaining your DREAM QUEST…a new exciting drive to drive yourself toward.

You know…you are your Life Programmer…
and Life Re-Programmer.

You (and you alone!) decide what you get to watch happen to you in your life, because you (and you alone!) are the only one who thinks your thoughts that make you then choose the people to be starring in your life…with their accompanying OFT TIMES VERY DARKLY DRAMATIC CIRCUMSTANCES!

IT'S YOUR PICKEROO WHAT YOU PROGRAM AND WATCH:

(A) Low-quality, trashy, negative, depressing belief programming

equals nothing good to watch happen in your life…and/or painful, trashy, depressing re-runs you are forced to watch happen… repeated again and again!

(B) High-quality, exciting, sexy, loving, feel-good belief programming equals fun, happy, high-quality stuff to watch happen…and the opportunity to watch these fun, happy, high-quality re-runs of wonderful times…repeated again and again!

When you think about all this belief programming stuff, you're reminded of something Carl Jung once said.

SOMETHING CARL JUNG ONCE SAID IN A BOX:

Carl Jung believed that we are all unwittingly searching for a Life Purpose (i.e., a Dream Quest). As Jung explained, if we don't have a Life Purpose/Dream Quest, we risk feeling that our lives are empty and meaningless. And because we don't want to feel all is for nothing, we find ourselves longing for some sort of something…an ANY-thing…just so we have some ADDICTIVE LONGING THING to focus on and give us a feeling of purpose. Unfortunately sometimes this ADDICTIVE LONGING THING is for a VERY LOW-LEVEL NEGATIVE LONGING THING…like drinking too many martinis, shoe shopping, gambling, drugging, cookie-ing, etc.…But luckily we people have a choice. Instead of settling for "a low-level negative longing thing," we can STOP it and SWAP it for a high-level Dream Quest!

Which brings you to…

LIFE LESSON #23

Often when you find yourself watching LOTS OF NEGATIVE CIRCUMSTANCES...

it's because your mind is seeking to bring you SOME SORT OF DRAMA, so your life doesn't feel empty and purposeless, so your mind starts to long for a Low-Level Quest!

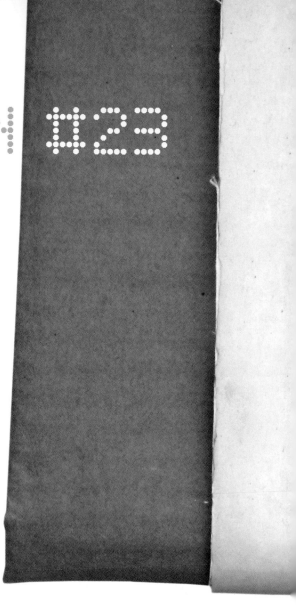

THE LOWDOWN ON LOW-LEVEL QUESTS:

If you're stuck watching PAIN-BEARING LOVE SCENES happen in your life… over and over…it's because some part of you BELIEVES it's meaningful/important/ fun/educational/rewarding/ exciting/distracting to watch these PAIN-BEARING LOVE SCENES so your life doesn't feel boring and purposeless!

Yes, some part of you believes that rather than have nothing to long for it's better to at least long for a LOW-LEVEL QUEST.

THANKFULLY, YOU NOW REALIZE:

YOU DON'T WANT TO RUN A LOW-LEVEL QUEST CONTEST AND WIN A LOW-LEVEL BUMMER OF A LIFE!

YOU WANT TO PROGRAM YOUR MIND SO IT RUNS A HIGH-LEVEL DREAM QUEST CONTEST…SO YOU CAN THEREBY WIN A HIGH-QUALITY, DREAM QUEST–BLOSSOMING, ALWAYS-GROWING LIFE.

Which brings you to…

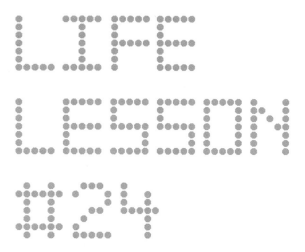

LIFE LESSON #24

Because you know that once you begin to think about your Dream Quest…you will always snag your Dream Quest…you know you must take some time to make sure that you have picked the right Dream Quest to think about.

You know some people get confused and rather than pick a DREAM QUEST based on the deep, internal desires of their heart, spirit, temperament, character…they pick an externally driven Dream Quest, like…

1. "I want to be a person who makes wads and wads of money."

2. "I want to be a person with lots of status and fame who doesn't have to wait in line in crowded restaurants to be seated."

Which brings you to…

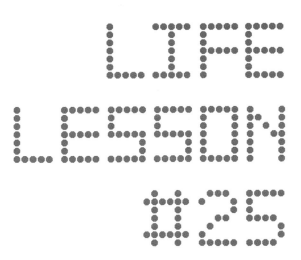

LIFE LESSON #25

WARNING:

EXTERNALLY DRIVEN PEOPLE
WILL ALWAYS CRASH AND BURN!

When folks foolishly pick a Dream
Quest based on external rewards...
rather than satisfying their true internal desires...
these externally driven people will remain
eternally unsatisfied...because THE FUN OF
EXTERNAL REWARDS EVENTUALLY FADES...
BUT INTERNAL REWARDS ARE FOREVER.

Thankfully you know better. You know to pick your Dream Quest wisely based on your true inner drive...

the deep, internal desires of your heart, spirit, temperament, character...
by subjecting yourself to...

THE DREAM QUEST
DETERMINATOR:

1. What would you do if you had unlimited time…like 1,000 years to live?

2. What would you do if you had limited time…like 1 year left to live?

3. What are you doing when you experience unlimited, time-flying time…when 10 hours feel like 1 hour?

4. What would you do if you had unlimited money?

5. What would you do if you had unlimited bravery?

Which brings you to…

LIFE LESSON #26

There's a thick line between knowing **and doing.**

Now that you know what the heck your Dream Quest is, you have to do whatever the hell you can **to snag it.**

HOW THE HELL TO SNAG YOUR DREAM QUEST:

1. Make a one-year plan. Write down everything you need to learn and do to snag your Dream Quest, then mark up your calendar with colorful daily, weekly, monthly goals. Update your progress daily! Rename this year to come THE YEAR I TOOK OVER THE WORLD!

2. Start an ENOUGH, DAMMIT SUPPORT GROUP…where you meet two to four times a month with two to four friends, to support and energize each other to keep going and growing.

3. Buy a Congratulations card and send it to yourself! Put it out on a bureau where you can see it daily. Envision lots more Congratulation cards arriving and surrounding it.

4. Shake up your life. Dye your hair! Move apartments! Move cities! Or try even shaking up your life in some small way. Pick a vice any vice to remove: coffee, alcohol, bread. When you make a change of any kind you are telling your subconscious: YO! I BE DA BOSS! I AM IN CHARGE OF MY LIFE AND CAN CHANGE IT FOR THE BETTER!

5. Boast and Post! Write a list of your best qualities and strongest spirit-given talents. Declare yourself to be a genius! Post this positive list in places you can see it.

6. Be patient. Just like it takes time for a flower or plant to grow and thrive, it will take time for you to see the new growth and new thriving in your life.

Which brings you to…

LIFE LESSON

#27

You must believe in
THE POWER OF
STOP AND SWAP
SWITCHEROO #3 of 5.

You must swap NEGATIVE blame for
POSITIVE self-responsibility…and try
to see your role in all your patterns
of pain, failure, and scarcity.

After all…if you don't take responsibility for your
patterns of bad stuff, then you lose your right to
take credit for your patterns of good stuff…and
no way do you want to lose that right.

The truth is: you're responsible for both the good
and bad.

When you think about your responsibility for the
bad, you think back to that spicy enchilada painful
time in your life…a time that you were very busy
trying to blame your pain on Tums…or Tom…
on anything or anyone but YOU and your
braindirtied cravings for self-destructive habits.

YOUR OLD MOTTO:

"I'M OKAY,
EVERYBODY ELSE SUCKS."

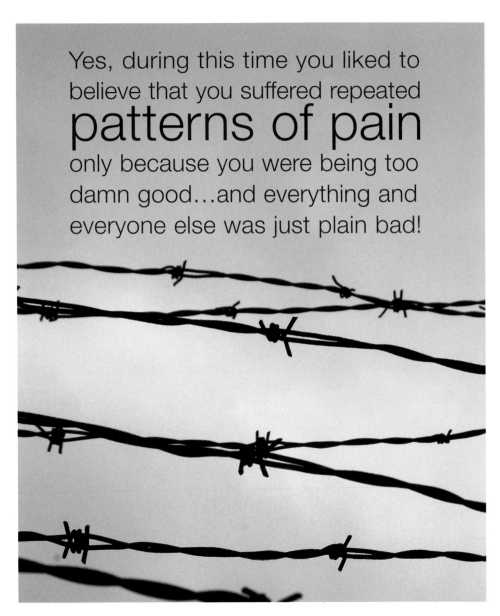

Yes, during this time you liked to believe that you suffered repeated **patterns of pain** only because you were being too damn good…and everything and everyone else was just plain bad!

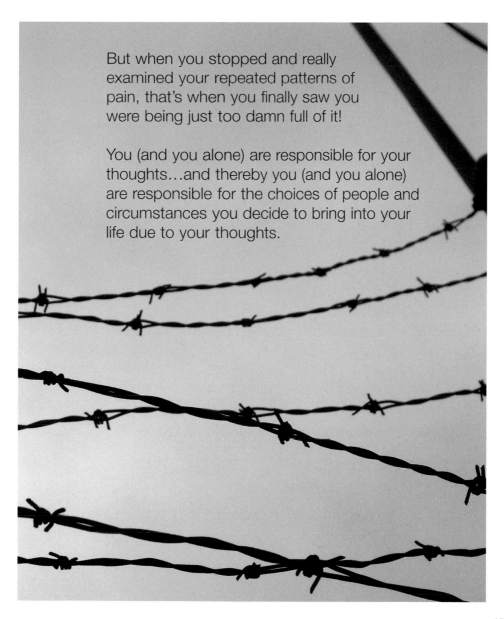

But when you stopped and really examined your repeated patterns of pain, that's when you finally saw you were being just too damn full of it!

You (and you alone) are responsible for your thoughts…and thereby you (and you alone) are responsible for the choices of people and circumstances you decide to bring into your life due to your thoughts.

The deal is this:

EAT ONE SPICY ENCHILADA AND FEEL PAIN…
AND YOU'RE ALLOWED TO CASH IN ONE "BLAME
THE ENCHILADA, BE RESPONSIBILITY-FREE" CARD.

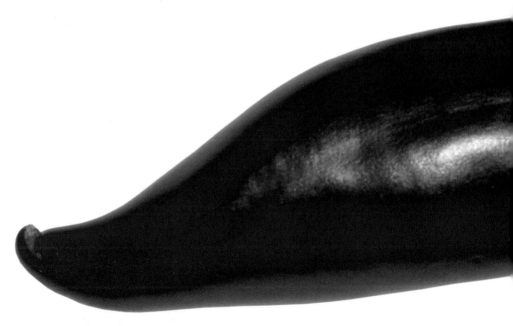

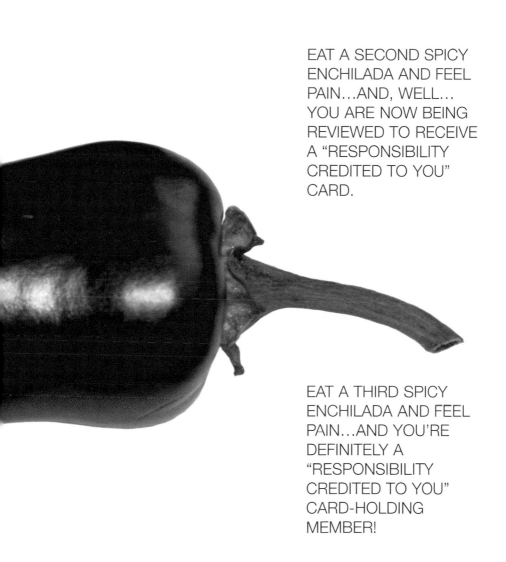

EAT A SECOND SPICY ENCHILADA AND FEEL PAIN…AND, WELL… YOU ARE NOW BEING REVIEWED TO RECEIVE A "RESPONSIBILITY CREDITED TO YOU" CARD.

EAT A THIRD SPICY ENCHILADA AND FEEL PAIN…AND YOU'RE DEFINITELY A "RESPONSIBILITY CREDITED TO YOU" CARD-HOLDING MEMBER!

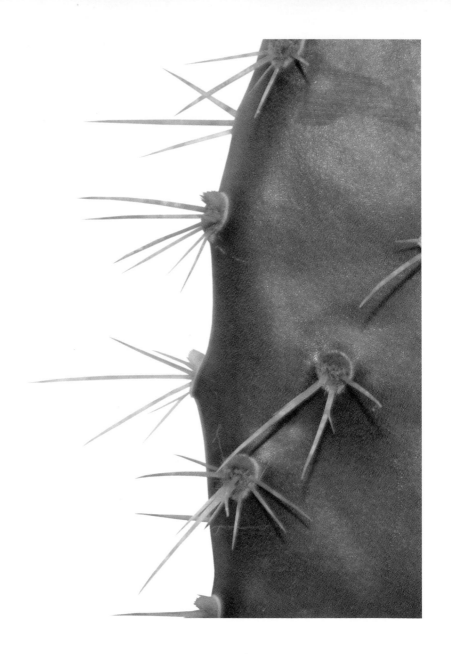

Whenever there's a pattern of pain, there's always a pattern of self-responsibility for your pain.

The Universe is NOT conspiring against you.

Bad luck is fiction. Self-responsibility is fact.

THE BAD NEWS IS:

When you finally face up to your role in your patterns of negative life circumstance, you will always feel that initial painful shock of truth and harsh glare of self-responsibility in your face.

THE BADDER NEWS IS:

Facing up to your self-responsibility means accepting MAYBE IT'S YOU, BUDDY/LADY… which then means it's then YOU (Yes, YOU!) (Not Tums!) (Not Tom!) who has to put in the effort of (Ugh!) change…which is why you've been clinging to blame.

THE GOOD NEWS IS:

The sooner you OWN your pattern of negative
life circumstances…the sooner you can
DISOWN IT…and thereby be on your way
to snagging your Dream Quest.

THE GOODER NEWS IS:

When you finally stop your pattern of blame,
you finally stop your annoying pattern of pain.

So…you gotta stop playing that Blame Game already!

You gotta stop saying:

My past is making me do it! My parents fed me enchiladas and taught me to eat enchiladas so I'm suffering now by wanting to eat them too.

You gotta start accepting:

Nothing in your past is in your physical reality right now making you do anything you don't choose to do...so why bother thinking about your past?

You are NOT your past actions.

You are NOT your past failures.

You are NOT how others have at one time treated you.

You are ONLY who you think you are right now in this moment.

You are ONLY what you do right now in this moment.

Which brings you to…

LIFE LESSON #28

If you want to
move forward,
you have to stop
looking backward…
and blaming your
past for all the pain,
failure, and scarcity
in your present.

"Poor me" is a poor excuse.
"Poor me" will only make you poorer and poorer.
Which reminds you of a good story about a
snake and a mistake.

A GOOD SNAKE MISTAKE STORY IN A BOX:
There once was a man who got bitten in the arm by
a poisonous snake. All he could think about was how
pissed off he was at this poisonous snake for biting him,
that he didn't relax so he could calmly see that he could
solve his problem (i.e., save his life) if he just stopped
being pissed and started sucking out the poison from
his arm. He died. End of story.

YOU KNOW THE IMPORTANT LESSON TO BE
LEARNED FROM THIS SNAKE MISTAKE:
Forgiveness truly is a logical
act of self interest.

Which brings you to…

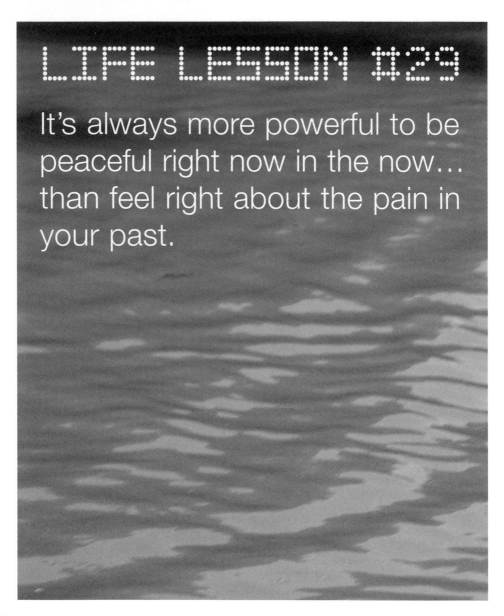

LIFE LESSON #29

It's always more powerful to be peaceful right now in the now... than feel right about the pain in your past.

Peacefulness

is power.

Peacefulness will always help you see answers and move forward. With this in mind, you decide to give yourself peace of mind...so you can be ensured of snagging a huge piece of that miracle pie.

DEUX PEACE OF MIND/PIECE OF MIRACLE PIE TECHNIQUES TO DO:

1. Take inventory of all the people you hate and resent…and consciously decide to forgive then forget them! Remind yourself: (a) When you resent someone you are giving this person control of your emotions! (b) When you respond with hate to hate, anger to anger, bitterness to bitterness, you are ironically becoming part of the problem. (c) When someone has behaved badly it's usually because they're "in the braindirtied dark." In fact, you should even send this person a little loving prayer that you hope they will some day soon clean off their braindirtied lens to the world.

2. Every time you find yourself thinking negative thoughts about blame and resentment, consciously ask yourself, "Am I thinking a dark thought that will stress me out? Not anymore! I will only think positive, bright thoughts that will relax me and illuminate my view of the world so I can lead a better life."

Which brings you to…

LIFE LESSON #30

You must believe in
THE POWER OF
STOP AND SWAP
SWITCHEROO #4 of 5.

You need to swap NEGATIVE doubt for POSITIVE faith…and fully convince yourself it is 100% possible to finally make your dreams come true!

You know thoughts of doubt can psych you out…and you've seen how this worked first hand…in Muhammad Ali's fist.

CHANTS ENCOUNTERS:

For weeks before that now famous Muhammad Ali vs. George Foreman boxing event, Muhammad Ali ranted all kinds of "thoughts of doubt to psych you out" chants at George Foreman… all meant to fill George with worries, empty him of faith. It worked. Georgie crumbled.

You must be a WARRIOR not a WORRIER...

You must make sure your braindirtied brain isn't ranting "thoughts of doubt to psych you out" when you're in the midst of pursuing your Dream Quest... thereby making you crumble.

You must ban all those NAUGHTY, NAUGHTY WORDS from your vocabulary…

I can't…I shouldn't… I'm worried that… I fear that…I doubt that…I don't believe that…Never…No way…Impossible…

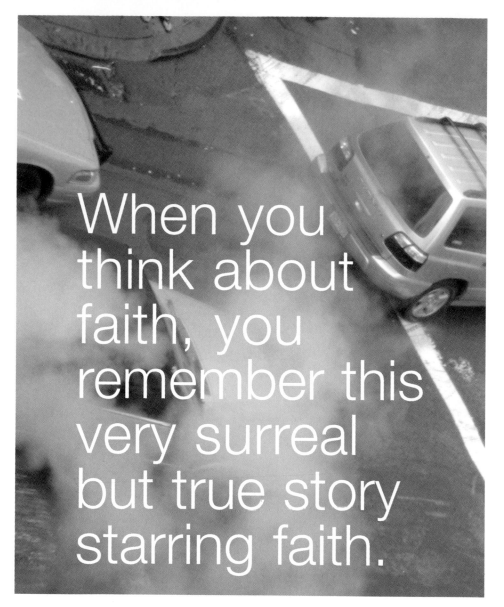

When you think about faith, you remember this very surreal but true story starring faith.

A VERY SURREAL BUT TRUE
STORY STARRING FAITH:

One afternoon you were moseying down the street when suddenly you saw this man standing by his car's steaming engine, yelling, "Faith! Faith! Where are you, faith?" as the smoke floated up from his engine. The next thing you knew, you heard this whiny, out-of-breath female voice behind you. "Relax, Sid, I'm coming!" You turned and saw a short, plump woman running toward him: Faith. You laughed. Although this was not what you had envisioned Faith to look like... she met Faith's description...ofttimes lagging, but there when you need Faith.

You know the lesson to be learned here:

The Universe will not always give you exactly what you want when you want...but as the famous saying goes, "God's delays are not God's denials."

Or as Thomas Edison once said, "Results? Why, man, I have gotten lots of results! If I find 10,000 ways something won't work, I haven't failed. I am not discouraged, because every wrong attempt discarded is often a step forward."

Which reminds you of…

LIFE LESSON #31

Just because something you want doesn't appear in your life right away, doesn't mean it's not on the delivery truck heading toward you…just a wee bit stuck in traffic…but soon to arrive yet.

You must tap into the power of "yet."
YET is a very powerful little big word.

There's only one letter difference between

YET
and
YES.

You must always have faith that your positive belief that a loving, happy, harmonious relationship with YOU IN IT does indeed exist...

and that your positive belief in its existence will ALWAYS eventually attract a loving, happy, harmonious relationship to you...

soon to arrive YET!

Which reminds you of something you need to remember…

LIFE LESSON #32

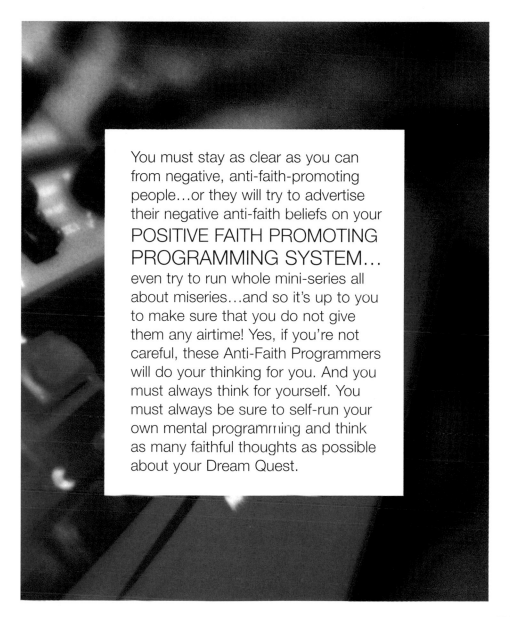

You must stay as clear as you can from negative, anti-faith-promoting people...or they will try to advertise their negative anti-faith beliefs on your **POSITIVE FAITH PROMOTING PROGRAMMING SYSTEM...** even try to run whole mini-series all about miseries...and so it's up to you to make sure that you do not give them any airtime! Yes, if you're not careful, these Anti-Faith Programmers will do your thinking for you. And you must always think for yourself. You must always be sure to self-run your own mental programming and think as many faithful thoughts as possible about your Dream Quest.

And whenever times appear dark, you thankfully know how to instantly reactivate disconnected faith with the following

EFFECTIVE VOICE COMMAND...

YOU MUST DECIDE NOW
AND REPEAT OUT LOUD:

"A lesser person would crumble right now! Not me! Because I'm the type of person who makes the world say YES to me!"

Which brings you to...

LIFE LESSON 033

A damn good attitude equals a damn good destiny.

And so with this in mind, you decide to keep your attitude perky **by practicing SIX EFFECTIVE FAITH ENERGIZERS:**

1. You follow two rules about complaining: (a) You're only allowed to complain about your life if it is really, really funny. (b) Your complaint must lead to a solution.

2. When lacking faith, GO JUMP IN THE OCEAN! Visit a beach or hike in the woods. By surrounding yourself by the miracle of nature, you'll be: (a) reminding your subconscious the world is infinite and complex…and thereby might offer infinite solutions to your situation and (b) recharging your emotional and physical batteries.

3. Play some inspiring music…anything from gospel to the Rolling Stones' "Under My Thumb"…whatever gets your heart pumping and your cajones revved back up.

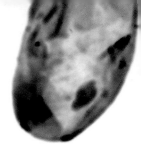

4. Find examples in magazines and on the Internet of people who snagged what you want. Plus in real life, try to surround yourself with people who have what you want. By seeing what you want is possible, you can train your brain to have faith that all is attainable.

5. Create a list of all the times you've gotten things you didn't think were getable. When faith is lagging, lug out this list.

6. Sit up straight and smile! Biologists have discovered that if you change your body carriage and facial expression to a more confident mode, you send messages to your brain that you are more confident, so you become more confident.

Which reminds you…

You must believe in **THE POWER OF STOP AND SWAP** SWITCHEROO #5 of 5.

You need to swap NEGATIVE laziness and apathy for POSITIVE enthusiastic discipline…and keep up your willpower to conquer your patterns of pain.

You know…wish though you may, The Universe does not reward the sneaky and lazy. (Would be nice if it did, eh?)

Unfortunately The Universe only rewards those who are willing to use disciplined persistence to overcome life's resistance…

and decidedly dump those negative beliefs once and for all.

Which brings you to…

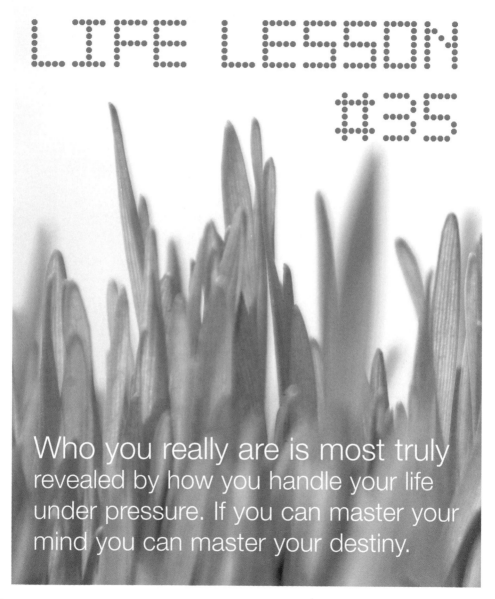

LIFE LESSON 036

Who you really are is most truly revealed by how you handle your life under pressure. If you can master your mind you can master your destiny.

SIMPLY PUT:

you must be ready to harness
the power of your inner strength
to accomplish two things...

1. HOLD UP YOUR STANDARDS!
(You must always make sure your standards remain stronger
than your impulses...and refuse to indulge in those tempting
learned cravings for those patterns of pain.)

2. CONTROL YOUR STIMULUS/RESPONSE MUSCLES!
(Whenever an obstacle, disappointment, failure, lion, tiger, or
bear enters your life...you must discipline your mind not to
think thoughts of panic or fear...but instead to think thoughts
of faith that you are the type of successful person who will
find a new, improved path to get you to your Dream Quest.)

Which brings you to...

LIFE LESSON #36

If you want to be the master of your destiny you must muster all of your **willpower.**

You must consistently, persistently self-run your mind so it stays focused on your Dream Quest and optimistic about attaining it.

You must decisively stop lazily heading down those same old familiar paths:

1. THE PATH OF LEAST RESISTANCE…
   that familiar road always traveled by your
   braindirtied subconscious…which will never
   lead you to your Dream Quest!

2. THE PATH OF MOST ASSISTANCE…
   the escape route away from feeling pain…
   via drugs, alcohol, work, shopping…
   which will never lead you to
   your Dream Quest!

Both of these two easy
paths might at first
glance look like they
will lead you to EASY
STREET. But in this
world, there is no such
thing as EASY STREET.
There is only discipline,
focus, and patience.

Which brings you to…

LIFE LESSON 137

Whenever you're caught up in a cycle of pain it's always because you're not using your will to self-run your mind…and instead, you are lazily choosing to stay spinning round and round in the same learned cycle of failure and hurt…

THE SAME FAMILIAR WHEEL OF MISFORTUNE.

BUT…it's always your choice…

WHEEL:

You can foolishly stay stuck in your cycle of learned habit…stuck on that wheel of familiar learned negative cravings, like a mouse on a wheel chasing cheese, spinning, spinning, spinning in non-motion, in non-satisfying-non-cheese-attainment…simply out of learned, lazy autopilot habit.

WILL:

You can use your will to get off that wheel
of familiar learned negative cravings…
and bravely head out on your own down
new paths to find lots of endless cheese…
find YOUR DREAM QUEST!

Of course heading out on your own is far scarier and requires far more energy in the long run, because…heck…finding your endless cheese/Dream Quest can be a very long run.

But jumping off that wheel of familiar learned negative cravings and bravely heading down new, unexplored paths will be the only way to ensure you'll ever find your endless cheese/Dream Quest.

Which brings you to…

LIFE LESSON #38

If you don't USE your
will eventually you will
LOSE your will.

THE DEAL IS THIS:
If you want buns of steel…
you must exercise your buns.
If you want discipline of steel…
you must exercise your discipline
to master your mind.

If you want to achieve only a little success in life… be ready to put in just a little discipline. If you want to achieve a lot of success…be ready to put in a lot of discipline.

Which brings you to…

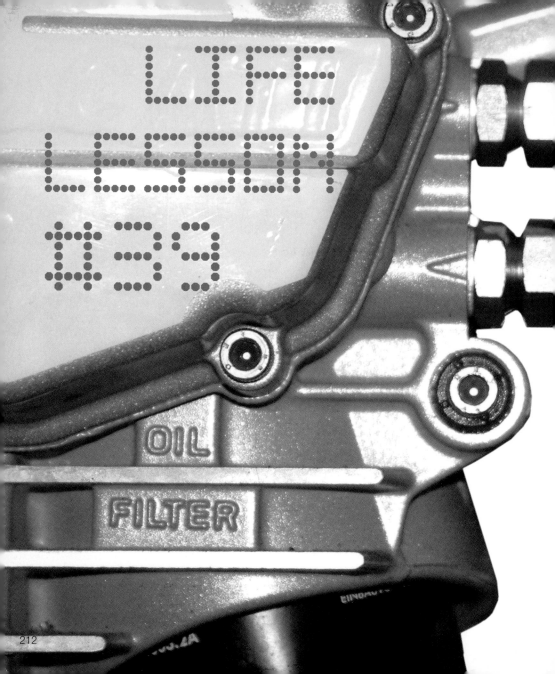

LIFE
LESSON
#39

OIL
FILTER

The more you increase
your willpower the more you
will increase your
"resultpower."

YOU KNOW:

the more intense your desire to
win, win, win = the stronger your

will to win, win, win.

SO:
increase your desirepower =
increase your willpower =
INCREASE YOUR RESULTPOWER!

Thankfully you know some...

RE-REV UP YOUR DESIREPOWER AND THEREBY RE-REV UP YOUR WILLPOWER SUREFIRE METHODS FOR SUCCESS:

1. ENJOY A MENTAL RENTAL: Close your eyes and imagine your life the way you want it. The more you watch this DREAM QUEST MENTAL RENTAL, the more you magnetize bringing it toward you.

2. ENJOY A WILLPOWER CHANT: Enough, dammit! Enough, dammit! Enough, dammit!

3. CONVINCE YOURSELF: SAME PROBLEM/DIFFERENT PERSON. Find someone else who has a similar problem as you, and help them...then your mind remembers, heck, it should be helping you too! Plus, when you become a teacher of how to solve your problem you are also unwittingly STOPPING and SWAPPING your identity from "victim of your problem" to "victor of your problem!"

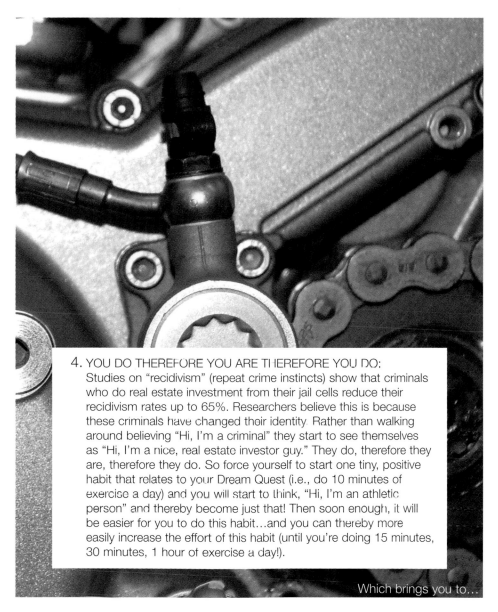

4. YOU DO THEREFORE YOU ARE THEREFORE YOU DO:
Studies on "recidivism" (repeat crime instincts) show that criminals who do real estate investment from their jail cells reduce their recidivism rates up to 65%. Researchers believe this is because these criminals have changed their identity. Rather than walking around believing "Hi, I'm a criminal" they start to see themselves as "Hi, I'm a nice, real estate investor guy." They do, therefore they are, therefore they do. So force yourself to start one tiny, positive habit that relates to your Dream Quest (i.e., do 10 minutes of exercise a day) and you will start to think, "Hi, I'm an athletic person" and thereby become just that! Then soon enough, it will be easier for you to do this habit…and you can thereby more easily increase the effort of this habit (until you're doing 15 minutes, 30 minutes, 1 hour of exercise a day!).

Which brings you to…

LIFE LESSON

#40

You must have one big goal for pain and failure: to be smart enough to always be suffering from new kinds of pain and failure.

Yes, you'll know you're making progress when you start making NEW mistakes.

New mistakes are a positive sign that you've successfully managed to say ENOUGH, DAMMIT to those familiar learned negative paths... and are bravely heading down new,

unexplored paths!

Which brings you to...

Pain and failure are here to stay!

You will always face some kind of pain and failure…even if you are happily rising up higher and higher on the evolutionary ladder.

BUT THE GOOD NEWS IS:

You now know how to deal with any and all pain and failure…thanks to your STOP AND SWAP SWITCHEROO SYSTEM…which reminds you of a good analogy.

A GOOD ANALOGY IN A BOX
Just like you can never cover the entire planet with leather…but you can wear leather sandals for a similar result… you can also never remove pain and failure from this planet…but you can at least always apply your STOP AND SWAP SWITCHEROO SYSTEM to them for a similar result.

Which brings you to…

LIFE
LESSON
042

Paul Cousineau was right: "Now is the time to live your ideal life."

Yes, this moment right here and now is a moment that you can use…and must use… to start living your ideal life.

Amazing as it is, this tiny moment offers you that great power.

So much so…the word *moment* should even be renamed *moment-um*…because it offers you the *momentum* to change your life.

IT'S YOUR CHOICE:

1. You can use this moment thinking negative thoughts about doubt, despair, blame, fear...which will then push you further away from love and success... with its negative energy moment-um!

OR

2. You can use this moment thinking positive thoughts about faith, harmony, abundance, love...which will then push you toward love and success...with its positive energy moment-um.

It's up to you to use every moment-um of your life wisely.

Which brings you to…

LIFE LESSON 043

You must practice the principles of this book consistently over time.

Repetition works.

Repetition works.

Repetition works.

Which brings you to…

LIFE LESSON 044

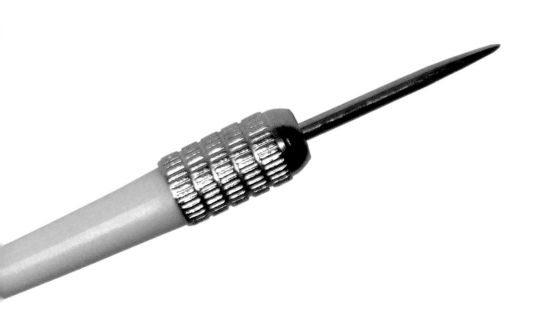

A HAPPY LIFE IS ALWAYS ABOUT YOUR
CONSISTENT ABILITY TO REDIRECT
YOUR MIND AWAY FROM THE NEGATIVE
AND TOWARD THE POSITIVE.

THERE IS A MAJOR CORRELATION

BETWEEN MASTERY OVER YOUR MIND

AND MASTERY OVER YOUR LIFE.

But heck, we
think by now
you've gotten

the point.

So...